The
Little Book
of
Gratitude
Quotes

ISBN-10: 057806586X
EAN-13: 9780578065861
LCCN: 2010905350

www.littlequotebooks.com

THE LITTLE QUOTE BOOKS

Classic · Simple · Inspiration

The
Little Book
of
Gratitude
Quotes

Edited by Kathleen Welton

Table of Contents

Thank You

With gratitude to those who have shared their favorite quotes with me over the years–and to the authors and teachers who came before us to record their classic, simple, and inspirational thoughts.

Introduction

$\mathcal{T}$his is a collection of 365 quotes—a quote to use as inspiration for each day of the year. Quotes have been selected to cover a dozen topics. They are arranged for easy access as follows:

- ❀ Appreciation
- ❀ Compassion
- ❀ Forgiveness
- ❀ Grace
- ❀ Gratitude
- ❀ Hope
- ❀ Joy
- ❀ Kindness
- ❀ Love
- ❀ Peace
- ❀ Success
- ❀ Wisdom

The quotes are arranged alphabetically by author in each section, so that you can easily find your favorite quotes by author and by topic.

These quotes—along with baseball cards, books, coins, and stamps—have been collected over the past 50 years. The best part of collecting things is to be able to take the time to look them over from time to time and then pass them on to someone else who will appreciate them. So it is now time to share my little collection of gratitude quotes. My hope is that this book will inspire a tradition for readers to collect their own quotes and even pass along some of their favorites.

Enjoy the journey!

Kathleen Welton
January 2011

Appreciation

❦

Far away there in the sunshine are my highest aspirations.
I may not reach them, but I can look up and see their beauty,
believe in them, and try to follow where they lead.

~ *Louisa May Alcott*

Take full account of the excellencies which you possess,
and in gratitude remember how
you would hanker after them, if you had them not.

~ *Marcus Aurelius*

When one door closes another door opens;
but we so often look so long and so regretfully upon
the closed door, that we do not see the ones which open for us.

~ *Alexander Graham Bell*

To everything there is a season,
and a time to every purpose under the heaven:
A time to be born, and a time to die;
a time to plant, and a time to pluck up that which is planted;

A time to kill, and a time to heal;
a time to break down, and a time to build up;
A time to weep, and a time to laugh;
a time to mourn, and a time to dance;
A time to cast away stones, and a time
to gather stones together;
a time to embrace, and a time to refrain from embracing;
A time to get, and a time to lose;
a time to keep, and a time to cast away;
A time to rend, and a time to sew;
a time to keep silence, and a time to speak;
A time to love, and a time to hate;
a time of war, and a time of peace.

~ *Bible, Ecclesiastes 3:1-8*

∾

What a miserable thing life is: you're living in clover, only
the clover isn't good enough.

~ *Bertolt Brecht*

∾

When the student is ready, the master appears.

~ *Buddha*

∾

Praise the bridge that carried you over.

~ *George Colman*

∾

Appreciation can make a day, even change a life.
Your willingness to put it into words is all that is necessary.

~ Margaret Cousins

∾

Reflect upon your present blessings,
of which every man has many—
not on your past misfortunes, of which all men have some.

~ Charles Dickens

∾

Luck is not chance—
It's Toil—
Fortune's expensive smile
Is earned–

~ Emily Dickinson

There is no Frigate like a Book
To take us Lands away
Nor any Coursers like a page
Of prancing Poetry–

~ Emily Dickinson

∾

There are only two ways to live your life.
One is as though nothing is a miracle.
The other is as though everything is a miracle.

~ Albert Einstein

∾

The first wealth is health.

~ *Ralph Waldo Emerson*

For each new morning with its light,
For rest and shelter of the night,
For health and food,
For love and friends,
For everything Thy goodness sends.

~ *Ralph Waldo Emerson*

༄

Learn to wish that everything should
come to pass exactly as it does.

~ *Epictetus*

༄

Go to foreign countries and you will get to know the good
things one possesses at home.

~ *Johann Wolfgang von Goethe*

༄

Only a stomach that rarely feels hungry
scorns common things.

~ Horace

∽

One looks back with appreciation to the brilliant teachers,
but with gratitude to those who touched our human feelings.
The curriculum is so much necessary raw material,
but warmth is the vital element for the growing plant
and for the soul of the child.

~ Carl Jung

∽

Beauty is truth, truth beauty,–that is all
Ye know on earth, and all ye need to know.

~ John Keats

∽

As we express our gratitude,
we must never forget that the highest appreciation
is not to utter words, but to live by them.

~ John Fitzgerald Kennedy

∽

For age is opportunity no less
Than youth itself, though in another dress,
And as the evening twilight fades away
The sky is filled with stars, invisible by day.

~ Henry Wadsworth Longfellow

∽

Yesterday is history. Tomorrow is a mystery.
And today? Today is a gift.
That's why we call it the present.

~ Babatunde Olatunji

∽

Beauty is in the eye of the beholder.

~ Proverb

∽

Not what we say about our blessings, but how we use them,
is the true measure of our thanksgiving.

~ W.T. Purkiser

∽

The future belongs to those who believe
in the beauty of their dreams.

~ Eleanor Roosevelt

∽

Be who you are and say what you feel because those who mind
don't matter and those who matter don't mind.

~ *Dr. Seuss*

∽

The butterfly counts not months but moments,
and has time enough.

~ *Rabindranath Tagore*

∽

A single gentle rain makes the grass many shades greener. So
our prospects brighten on the influx of better thoughts.

~ *Henry David Thoreau*

∽

When I let go of what I am, I become what I might be.

~ *Lao Tzu*

∽

Enjoy the little things in life, for one day you may look back
and realize they were the big things.

~ *Author Unknown*

∽

We can only be said to be alive in those moments when our hearts are conscious of our treasures.

~ *Thornton Wilder*

Compassion

May I and all beings
be filled with lovingkindness.
May I and all beings
be safe from inner and outer dangers.
May I and all beings
be well in body and mind.
May I and all beings
be happy and free.

~ Buddhist Meditation

Wisdom, compassion, and courage are the three universally
recognized moral qualities of men.

~ Confucius

When we see men of worth,
we should think of equaling them;
when we see men of a contrary character,
we should turn inwards and examine ourselves.

~ Confucius

One's life has value so long as one attributes value to
the life of others, by means of love, friendship,
indignation and compassion.

~ *Simone de Beauvoir*

∾

Anger as soon as fed is dead—
'Tis starving makes it fat—

~ *Emily Dickinson*

∾

Do first things first, and second things not at all.

~ *Peter Drucker*

∾

A question that sometime drives me hazy:
am I or are the others crazy?

~ *Albert Einstein*

Our task must be to free ourselves by widening our
circle of compassion to embrace all living creatures
and the whole of nature and its beauty.

~ *Albert Einstein*

∾

The purpose of life is not to be happy. It is to be useful,
to be honorable, to be compassionate, to have it make some
difference that you have lived and lived well.

~ Ralph Waldo Emerson

Parents can only give good advice or put them on
the right paths, but the final forming of a person's
character lies in their own hands.

~ Anne Frank

Doubt is a pain too lonely to know that faith is his twin brother.

~ Kahlil Gibran

And so long as you haven't experienced
this: to die and so to grow,
you are only a troubled guest
on the dark earth.

~ John Wolfgang von Goethe

Anger is a momentary madness, so control
your passion or it will control you.

~ Horace

∞

Alone we can do so little; together we can do so much.

~ Helen Keller

∞

An individual has not started living until he can rise
above the narrow confines of his individualistic
concerns to the broader concerns of all humanity.

~ Martin Luther King, Jr.

∞

Meditation is not the means to an end.
It is both the means and the end.

~ Jiddu Krisnamurti

∞

He has the right to criticize who has the heart to help.

~ Abraham Lincoln

Am I not destroying my enemies when I make friends of them?

~ Abraham Lincoln

∞

Be still, sad heart! And cease repining;
Behind the clouds is the sun still shining,
Thy fate is the common fate of all,
Into each life some rain must fall,
Some days must be dark and dreary.

~ Henry Wadsworth Longfellow

If we could read the secret history of our enemies,
we should find in each man's life sorrow and suffering
enough to disarm all hostility.

~ Henry Wadsworth Longfellow

∽

One can spend a lifetime assigning blame, finding the cause
"out there" for all the troubles that exist. Contrast this
with the "responsible attitude" of confronting the situation,
bad or good, and instead of asking "What caused the trouble?
Who was to blame?" asking "How can I handle this present
situation to make the most of it? What can I salvage here?"

~ Abraham Maslow

∽

O God and Heavenly Father. Grant to us the
serenity of mind to accept that which cannot be
changed; the courage to change that which can be
changed, and the wisdom to know the one from the other.

~ Reinhold Niebuhr

∽

The real voyage of discovery consists not in seeking new
landscapes but in having new eyes.

~ Marcel Proust

The unexamined life is not worth living.

~ Socrates

Perpetual devotion to what a man calls his business, is only to
be sustained by perpetual neglect of many other things.

~ Robert Louis Stevenson

The best way to cheer yourself up is to cheer somebody else up.

~ Mark Twain

I have just three things to teach: simplicity, patience,
compassion. These three are your greatest treasures.

~ Lao Tzu

Whatever is to be will be!

~ Author Unknown

Forgiveness

The kingdom of God is within you.

~ *Bible, Luke, 17:21*

It is easier to forgive an enemy than to forgive a friend.

~ *William Blake*

Great things are done when men and mountains meet.

~ *William Blake*

Holding on to anger is like grasping a hot coal with the intent of throwing it at someone else; you are the one who gets burned.

~ *Buddha*

Love yourself—accept yourself—forgive yourself—
and be good to yourself,
because without you the rest of us are without a
source of many wonderful things.

~ Leo F. Buscaglia

❧

We make a living by what we get, but we make a life by
what we give.

~ Winston Churchill

❧

Never does the human soul appear so strong as when it foregoes
revenge and dares to forgive an injury.

~ Edwin Hubbell Chapin

❧

It has long been an axiom of mine that the little things are
infinitely the most important.

~ Sir Arthur Conan Doyle

❧

The responsibility of tolerance lies with those who
have the wider vision.

~ George Eliot

❧

You cannot do a kindness too soon, for you never know how soon it will be too late.

~ *Ralph Waldo Emerson*

༄

The weak can never forgive.
Forgiveness is the attribute of the strong.

~ *Mahatma Gandhi*

༄

Find the good and praise it.

~ *Alex Haley*

༄

He that cannot forgive others, breaks the bridge over which he himself must pass if he would ever reach heaven; for everyone has need to be forgiven.

~ *George Herbert*

༄

An individual who breaks a law that conscience tells him is unjust, and who willingly accepts the penalty of imprisonment in order to arouse the conscience of the community over its injustice, is in reality expressing the highest respect for the law.

~ *Martin Luther King, Jr.*

༄

What is necessary to change a person is to change
his awareness of himself.

~ *Abraham Maslow*

∾

Forgiveness is the final form of love.

~ *Reinhold Niebuhr*

∾

What doesn't kill us makes us stronger.

~ *Friedrich Nietzsche*

∾

To err is human, to forgive divine.

~ *Alexander Pope*

∾

It is better to light a candle than curse the darkness.

~ *Chinese Proverb*

∾

Once the game is over, the king and the pawn go back in
the same box.

~ *Italian Proverb*

∾

The future enters into us, in order to transform itself in us,
long before it happens.

~ Rainer Maria Rilke

∽

To-day's your natal day,
Sweet flowers I bring;
Mother, accept, I pray,
My offering.

And may you happy live,
And long us bless;
Receiving as you give
Great happiness.

~ Christina Rossetti

∽

Be faithful in small things because it is in them
that your strength lies.

~ Mother Teresa

∽

Let us forgive each other—only then will we live in peace.
~ Leo Tolstoy

∽

Forgiveness is the fragrance that the violet sheds on the heel
that has crushed it.

~ Mark Twain

∽

Forgiveness is giving up the idea that the past could
have had different results.

~ Author Unknown

Letting go doesn't mean giving up, but rather accepting that
there are things that cannot be.

~ Author Unknown

To understand all is to forgive all.

~ Voltaire

Forgiveness is a funny thing. It warms the heart and
cools the sting.

~ William Arthur Ward

The strongest and sweetest songs yet remain to be sung.

~ Walt Whitman

After a good dinner one can forgive anybody, even
one's own relations.

~ Oscar Wilde

Grace

❦

You say grace before meals. All right. But I say grace before
the concert and the opera, and grace before the play and panto-
mime, and grace before I open a book, and grace before sketch-
ing, painting, swimming, fencing, boxing, walking, playing,
dancing and grace before I dip the pen in the ink.

~ *G.K. Chesterton*

Attitude is a little thing that makes a big difference.

~ *Winston Churchill*

Courtesies of a small and trivial character are the ones which
strike deepest in the grateful and appreciating heart.

~ *Henry Clay*

Our deeds determine us, as much as we determine our deeds.

~ *George Eliot*

Accept the place the divine providence has found for you, the society of your contemporaries, the connection of events.

~ *Ralph Waldo Emerson*

෬

Gratitude is a quality similar to electricity: it must be produced and discharged and used up in order to exist at all.

~ *William Faulkner*

෬

Well done is better than well said.

~ *Benjamin Franklin*

෬

To go with the drift of things,
To yield with a grace to reason,
And bow and accept the end
Of a love or a season?

~ *Robert Frost*

The best way out is always through.

~ *Robert Frost*

෬

Whatever you can do or dream you can, begin it. Boldness has
genius, power and magic in it!

~ *Johann Wolfgang von Goethe*

∽

It matters not how strait the gate,
How charged with punishments the scroll.
I am the master of my fate:
I am the captain of my soul.

~ *William Ernest Henley*

∽

The hardest arithmetic to master is that
which enables us to count our blessings.

~ *Eric Hoffer*

∽

Neither smiles nor frowns, neither good intentions
nor harsh words, are a substitute for strength.

~ *John F. Kennedy*

∽

Be bold—and mighty forces will come to your aid.

~ *Basil King*

∽

If you can keep your head when all about you
Are losing theirs and blaming it on you...
If you can meet with Triumph and Disaster
And treat those two imposters the same...
Yours is the Earth and everything that's in it,
And—which is more—you'll be a Man, my son!

~ *Rudyard Kipling*

∽

In character, in manners, in style, in all things,
the supreme excellence is simplicity.

~ *Henry Wadsworth Longfellow*

∽

Amazing grace! (how sweet the sound!)
That sav'd a wretch like me!
I once was lost, but now am found;
Was blind, but now I see.

'Twas grace that taught my heart to fear,
And grace my fears reliev'd;
How precious did that grace appear,
The hour I first believ'd!

~ *John Newton*

∽

Where I was born and where and how I have lived is unimportant. It is what I have done with where I have been that should be of interest.

~ *Georgia O'Keefe*

◌

You will go most safely by the middle way.

~ *Ovid*

◌

Miracles are instantaneous—they cannot be summoned, but come of themselves, usually at unlikely moments and to those who least expect them.

~ *Katherine Anne Porter*

◌

When eating bamboo sprouts, remember the man who planted them.

~ *Chinese Proverb*

Nature, time, and patience are the three great physicians.

~ *Proverb*

◌

At times our own light goes out and is rekindled by a spark from another person. Each of us has cause to think with deep gratitude of those who have lighted the flame within us.

~ *Albert Schweitzer*

∾

To be or not to be; that is the question:
Whether 'tis nobler in the mind to suffer
The slings and arrows of outrageous fortune,
Or to take arms against a sea of troubles,
And by opposing end them?

~ *William Shakespeare*

∾

There are two kinds of people in the world: those who come into a room and say, "Here I am!" and those who come in and say, "Ah, there you are!"

~ *Author Unknown*

Hem your blessings with thankfulness so they don't unravel.

~ *Author Unknown*

∾

Endure, and preserve yourself for better things.

~ *Virgil*

∾

Each player must accept the cards life deals him or her: but once they are in hand, he or she alone must decide how to play the cards in order to win the game.

~ Voltaire

Feeling gratitude and not expressing it is like wrapping a present and not giving it.

~ William Arthur Ward

It's the little details that are vital. Little things make big things happen.

~ John Wooden

Gratitude

The unthankful heart... discovers no mercies; but let the thankful heart sweep through the day and, as the magnet finds the iron, so it will find, in every hour, some heavenly blessings!

~ Henry Ward Beecher

Be anxious for nothing, but in everything by prayer and supplication, with thanksgiving, let your requests be made known to God.

~ Bible, Philippians 4:6

There is no greater difference between men than between grateful and ungrateful people.

~ Reginald Horace Blyth

Let us rise up and be thankful, for if we didn't learn a lot today, at least we learned a little, and if we didn't learn a little, at least we didn't get sick, and if we got sick, at least we didn't die; so, let us all be thankful.

~ Buddha

⌒◦

When our perils are past, shall our gratitude sleep?

~ George Canning

⌒◦

When we were children we were grateful to those who filled our stockings at Christmas time. Why are we not grateful to God for filling our stockings with legs?

~ G.K. Chesterton

I would maintain that thanks are the highest form of thought; and that gratitude is happiness doubled by wonder.

~ G.K. Chesterton

⌒◦

Gratitude is not only the greatest of virtues, but the parent of all others.

~ Cicero

⌒◦

I'm Nobody! Who are you?
Are you—Nobody too?

~ Emily Dickinson

∽

I feel a very unusual sensation—if it is not
indigestion, I think it must be gratitude.

~ Benjamin Disraeli

∽

If you have lived, take thankfully the past.

~ John Dryden

∽

If the only prayer you said in your whole life was,
"thank you," that would suffice.

~ Meister Eckhart

∽

I awoke this morning with devout thanksgiving for my friends,
the old and the new.

~ Ralph Waldo Emerson

∽

God helps those who help themselves.

~ *Benjamin Franklin*

∽

In the sweetness of friendship let there be laughter, and sharing of pleasures. For in the dew of little things the heart finds its morning and is refreshed.

~ *Kahlil Gibran*

∽

Wake at dawn with a winged heart and give thanks for another day of loving.

~ *Kahlil Gibran*

∽

Thou hast given so much to me,
Give one thing more, - a grateful heart;
Not thankful when it pleaseth me,
As if Thy blessings had spare days,
But such a heart whose pulse may be Thy praise.

~ *George Herbert*

∽

Most human beings have an almost infinite capacity for taking things for granted.

~ *Aldous Huxley*

∽

Gratitude is merely the secret hope of further favors.

~ *François Duc de la Rochefoucauld*

∾

The moment one gives close attention to anything, even a blade of grass, it becomes a mysterious, awesome, indescribably magnificent world in itself.

~ *Henry Miller*

∾

Thanks are justly due for boons unbought.

~ *Ovid*

∾

Let us be grateful to people who make us happy; they are the charming gardeners who make our souls blossom.

~ *Marcel Proust*

∾

Who does not thank for little will not thank for much.

~ *Estonian Proverb*

∾

To educate yourself for the feeling of gratitude means
to take nothing for granted, but to always seek out and
value the kind that will stand behind the action.
Nothing that is done for you is a matter of course.
Everything originates in a will for the good, which is directed
at you. Train yourself never to put off the word or action for the
expression of gratitude.

~ *Albert Schweitzer*

∽

The grateful person, being still the most severe exacter of himself, not only confesses, but proclaims, his debts.

~ **Robert South**

∽

Silent gratitude isn't much use to anyone.

~ *G.B. Stern*

∽

No duty is more urgent than that of returning thanks.

~ Author Unknown

Gratitude is the best attitude.

~ Author Unknown

Gratitude can turn a negative into a positive.
Find a way to be thankful for your troubles
and they can become your blessings.

~ Author Unknown

∽

God gave you a gift of 86,400 seconds today. Have you used
one to say "thank you?"

~ William Arthur Ward

∽

But the value of gratitude does not consist solely in
getting you more blessings in the future. Without gratitude
you cannot long keep from dissatisfied thought regarding
things as they are.

~ Wallace Wattles

Hope

⌖

If it is not right do not do it; if it is not true do not say it.

~ Marcus Aurelius

All that we are is a result of what have thought. If a man speaks or acts with an evil thought, pain follows him. If a man speaks or acts with a pure thought, happiness follows him, like a shadow that never leaves him.

~ Budda

"Hope" is the thing with feathers—
That perches in the soul—
And sings the tune without the words—
And never stops—at all—

~ Emily Dickinson

By Chivalries as tiny,
A Blossom, or a Book,
The seeds of smiles are planted—
Which blossom in the dark.

~ Emily Dickinson

Truth is such a rare thing, it is delightful to tell it.

~ Emily Dickinson

∽

The best way to predict the future is to create it.

~ Peter Drucker

∽

Learn from yesterday, live for today, hope for tomorrow.
~ Albert Einstein

Logic will get you from A to B. Imagination will
take you everywhere.

~ Albert Einstein

A man should look for what is, and not for what he
thinks should be.

~ Albert Einstein

∽

We shall not cease from exploration
At the end of all our exploring
Will be to arrive where we started
And know the place for the first time.

~ T.S. Eliot

∽

A ship ought not to be held by one anchor,
nor life by a single hope.

~ Epictetus

∽

Never leave that till tomorrow which you can do today.

~ Benjamin Franklin

∽

Two roads diverged in a wood, and I—
I took the one less traveled by,
And that has made all the difference.

~ Robert Frost

∽

If we cannot secure all our rights, let us secure
what we can.

~ Thomas Jefferson

∽

We should not let our fears hold us back from pursuing
our hopes.

~ *John F. Kennedy*

∽

I have a dream that my four little children will one day live in a
nation where they will not be judged by the color of their skin,
but by the content of their character.

~ *Martin Luther King, Jr.*

Everything that is done in the world is done by hope.

~ *Martin Luther King, Jr.*

I say to you today, my friends, that in spite of the difficulties
and frustrations of the moment, I still have a dream.

~ *Dr. Martin Luther King, Jr.*

∽

The setting of a great hope is like the setting of the sun.
The brightness of our life is gone.

~ *Henry Wadsworth Longfellow*

∽

that you're not free
until you've been made captive by
supreme belief—credulity

~ *Marianne Moore*

∽

Hope springs eternal in the human breast;
Man never is, but always to be blest.

~ *Alexander Pope*

∽

From intention springs the deed,
from the deed springs the
habits. From the habits grow the character, from
character develops destiny.

~ *Chinese Proverb*

Hope for the best but prepare for the worst.

~ *English Proverb*

The road to hell is paved with good intentions.

~ *Proverb*

∽

Honesty is the best policy. If I lose mine honor,
I lose myself.

~ *William Shakespeare*

∽

If you tell the truth you don't have to
remember anything.

~ *Mark Twain*

∽

A journey of a thousand miles begins with a single step.

~ *Lao Tzu*

Truth fears no questions.

~ *Author Unknown*

Hope sees the invisible, feels the intangible and achieves the impossible.

~ *Author Unknown*

Friends are angels who lift us to our feet when our wings have trouble remembering how to fly.

~ *Author Unknown*

Joy

Blessed are those that can give without remembering and
take without forgetting.

~ *Elizabeth Bibesco*

It is the supreme art of the teacher to awaken
joy in creative expression and knowledge.

~ *Albert Einstein*

The ideals which have always shone before me
and filled me with the joy
of living are goodness, beauty, and truth.

~ *Albert Einstein*

Whenever you are sincerely pleased, you are nourished.

~ *Ralph Waldo Emerson*

There is no beautifier of complexion, or form, or behavior, like
the wish to scatter joy and not pain around us.

~ *Ralph Waldo Emerson*

Seek not good from without: seek it from within yourselves, or you will never find it.

~ Epictetus

∽

Joy is not in things, it is in us.

~ Benjamin Franklin

A place for everything, everything in its place.

~ Benjamin Franklin

∽

You pray in your distress and in your need; would that you might also pray in the fullness of your joy and in the days of your abundance.

~ Kahlil Gibran

∽

One ought, every day at least, to hear a little song, read a good poem, see a fine picture, and if it were possible, to speak a few reasonable words.

~ Johann Wolfgang von Goethe

The person born with a talent they are meant to use will find their greatest happiness in using it.

~ Johann Wolfgang von Goethe

∽

Happiness is a butterfly which, when pursued, is always just beyond your grasp but which, if you will sit down quietly, may alight upon you.

~ Nathaniel Hawthorne

We hold these truths to be self-evident, that all men are created equal, that they are endowed by their Creator with certain unalienable Rights, that among these are Life, Liberty, and the pursuit of Happiness.

~ Thomas Jefferson

The best and most beautiful things in the world cannot be seen or even touched. They must be felt with the heart.

~ Helen Keller

The life of a man consists not in seeing visions and in dreaming dreams, but in active charity and in willing service.

~ Henry Wadsworth Longfellow

One joy scatters a hundred griefs.

~ Chinese Proverb

Unshared joy is an unlighted candle.

~ Spanish Proverb

Happiness is not a goal; it is a by-product.

~ *Eleanor Roosevelt*

Since you get more joy out of giving joy to others, you should put a good deal of thought into the happiness that you are able to give.

~ *Eleanor Roosevelt*

∽

Things won are done, joy's soul lies in the doing.

~ *William Shakespeare*

∽

Joy is a net of love by which you can catch souls.

~ *Mother Teresa*

∽

It's noble to be good, and it's nobler to teach others to be good, and less trouble.

~ *Mark Twain*

Always do right—this will gratify some and astonish the rest.

~ *Mark Twain*

∽

He who knows that enough is enough will always have enough.

~ *Lao Tzu*

When the best leader's work is done the people say,
"we did it ourselves."

~ *Lao Tzu*

∞

Gratitude can transform common days into thanksgivings, turn
routine jobs into joy, and change ordinary opportunities
into blessings.

~ *William Arthur Ward*

∞

Talent is God given. Be humble. Fame is man-given. Be grateful. Conceit is self-given. Be careful.

~ *John Wooden*

It's what you learn after you know it all that counts.

~ *John Wooden*

∞

•

I wandered lonely as a cloud
That floats on high o'er vales and hills,
When all at once I saw a crowd,
A host, of golden daffodils;
Beside the lake, beneath the trees,
Fluttering and dancing in the breeze.

~ *William Wordsworth*

When you are old and grey and full of sleep,
And nodding by the fire, take down this book,
And slowly read, and dream of the soft look
Your eyes had once, and of their shadows deep;

~ *William Butler Yeats*

I have spread my dreams under your feet; Tread softly because
you tread on my dreams.

~ *William Butler Yeats*

Kindness

Gratitude is the fairest blossom which springs from the soul.

~ *Henry Ward Beecher*

A faithful friend is the medicine of life.

~ *Bible, Ecclesiasticus 6:16*

Do to others as you would have them do to you.

~ *Bible, Luke 6:31*

The greatest protection in all the world is lovingkindness.

~ *Buddha*

Forget injuries, never forget kindnesses.

~ *Confucius*

Act with kindness, but do not expect gratitude.

~ *Confucius*

I know not how to thank you…To give delight is hallowed—
perhaps the toil of angels, whose avocations are concealed.

~ *Emily Dickinson*

❧

What do we live for, if it is not to make life less difficult to
each other?

~ *George Eliot*

❧

The only way to have a friend is to be one.

~ *Ralph Waldo Emerson*

❧

Truth is a deep kindness that teaches us to be content in our
everyday life and share with the people the same happiness.

~ *Kahlil Gibran*

❧

Kindness is the golden chain by which society is
bound together.

~ *Johann Wolfgang von Goethe*

❧

Generosity is the flower of justice.

~ *Nathaniel Hawthorne*

❧

Kindness can become its own motive. We are made
kind by being kind.

~ *Eric Hoffer*

❧

The time is always right to do what is right.

~ *Martin Luther King, Jr.*

❧

Give me your tired, your poor,
Your huddled masses yearning to breathe free,
The wretched refuse of your teeming shore.
Send these, the homeless, tempest-tost to me,
I lift my lamp beside the golden door!

~ *Emma Lazarus*

❧

Always be kind, for everyone is fighting a hard battle.

~ *Plato*

❧

Kindness begets kindness.

~ *Greek Proverb*

❧

Blessed is he who speaks a kindness; thrice blessed is
he who repeats it.

~ *Arabian Proverb*

One can pay back the loan of gold, but one dies forever in debt
to those who are kind.

~ *Malayan Proverb*

൭

Two kinds of gratitude: The sudden kind we feel for what we
take; the larger kind we feel for what we give.

~ *Edwin Arlington Robinson*

൭

Friendship with oneself is all-important, because without it one
cannot be friends with anyone else in the world.

~ *Eleanor Roosevelt*

൭

The most I can do for my friend is simply to be his friend. I
have no wealth to bestow on him. If he knows that I am happy
in loving him, he will want no other reward. Is not friendship
divine in this?

~ *Henry David Thoreau*

൭

Kindness is the language which the deaf can hear and the blind can see.

~ Mark Twain

∾

Answer with kindness when faced with hostility.

~ Lao Tzu

Kindness in words creates confidence. Kindness in thinking creates profoundness. Kindness in giving creates love.

~ Lao Tzu

∾

A friend is someone who knows you well and still likes you.

~ Author Unknown

A person can have no better epitaph than that which is inscribed in the hearts of his friends.

~ Author Unknown

∾

A warm smile is the universal language of kindness.

~ William Arthur Ward

∾

Do you wish the world were happy?
Then remember day by day
Just to scatter seeds of kindness
As you pass along the way,
For the pleasures of the many
May be ofttimes traced to one,
As the hand that plants an acorn
Shelters armies from the sun.

~ Ella Wheeler Wilcox

So many gods, so many creeds,
So many paths that wind and wind,
While just the art of being kind
Is all the sad world needs.

~ Ella Wheeler Wilcox

On that best portion of a good man's life,
His little nameless, unremembered, acts
Of kindness and of love.

~ William Wordsworth

Love

Whoso loves
Believes the impossible.

~ *Elizabeth Barrett Browning*

How do I love thee? Let me count the ways.
I love thee to the depth and breadth and height
My soul can reach, when feeling out of sight
For the ends of being and ideal grace.

~ *Elizabeth Barrett Browning*

So, fall asleep love, loved by me....for I know love, I am
loved by thee.

~ *Robert Browning*

Love dies only when growth stops.

~ *Pearl S. Buck*

But to see her was to love her;
Love but her, and love forever.

~ *Robert Burns*

∾

When it comes to life the critical thing is whether you take
things for granted or take them with gratitude.

~ *G.K. Chesterton*

∾

To love a thing means wanting it to live.

~ *Confucius*

∾

Honor the ocean of love.

~ *George de Benneville*

∾

A loving heart is the truest wisdom.

~ *Charles Dickens*

∾

If I can stop one Heart from breaking
I shall not live in vain
If I can ease one Life the Aching
Or cool one Pain

Or help one fainting Robin
Unto his Nest again
I shall not live in Vain.

~ *Emily Dickinson*

∾

The magic of first love is our ignorance that it can ever end.

~ *Benjamin Disraeli*

∾

The golden moments in the stream of life rush past us and we
see nothing but sand; the angels come to visit us, and we only
know them when they are gone.

~ *George Eliot*

∾

O Divine Master, grant that I may not so much
seek to be consoled as to console;
To be understood as to understand;
To be loved as to love.

~ *Saint Francis of Assisi*

∾

Immature love says: I love you because I need you.
Mature love says: I need you because I love you.

~ *Erich Fromm*

Love has nothing to do with what you are expecting to get—only
with what you are expecting to give—which is everything.

~ *Katharine Hepburn*

Love is like a beautiful flower which I may not touch,
but whose fragrance makes the garden a place of delight
just the same.

~ *Helen Keller*

What we have once enjoyed we can never lose. All that we love
deeply becomes a part of us.

~ *Helen Keller*

The madness of love is the greatest of heaven's blessings.

~ *Plato*

At the touch of love everyone becomes a poet...

~ *Plato*

The greatest love is a mother's; then comes a dog's; then comes a sweetheart's.

~ *Polish Proverb*

ᘒ

The work of the eyes is done. Go now and do the heart-work on the images imprisoned within you.

~ *Rainer Maria Rilke*

Be patient toward all that is unsolved in your heart and try to love the questions themselves... like books that are written in a foreign language. Do not seek the answers, which cannot be given to you because you would not be able to live them. And the point is to live everything. Live the questions now... Resolve to be always beginning–to be a beginner.

~ *Rainer Maria Rilke*

ᘒ

They do not love that do not show their love.

~ *William Shakespeare*

ᘒ

Shall I compare thee to a summer's day? Thou art more lovely and more temperate.

~ *William Shakespeare*

ᘒ

'Tis better to have loved and lost
Than never to have loved at all.

~ *Alfred Lord Tennyson*

༉

Sing like no one's listening, love like you've never been hurt,
dance like nobody's watching, and live like it's heaven on earth.

~ *Mark Twain*

༉

Being deeply loved by someone gives you strength; loving
someone deeply gives you courage.

~ *Lao Tzu*

༉

Some people come into our lives,
Leave footprints in our hearts,
And we are never ever the same.

~ *Author Unknown*

༉

Love conquers all things; let us surrender to love.

~ *Virgil*

༉

To love oneself is the beginning of a lifelong romance.

~ *Oscar Wilde*

Peace

❧

Life appears to me too short to be spent in
nursing animosity, or registering wrongs.

~ *Charlotte Brontë*

Less is more.

~ *Robert Browning*

If a man speaks or acts with a pure thought, happiness follows
him like a shadow that never leaves him.

~ *Buddha*

We never know how high we are
Till we are called to rise.

~ *Emily Dickinson*

Finish each day and be done with it. You have done what you could; some blunders and absurdities have crept in; forget them as soon as you can. Tomorrow is a new day; you shall begin it serenely and with too high a spirit to be encumbered with your old nonsense.

~ Ralph Waldo Emerson

Nothing can bring you peace but yourself.

~ Ralph Waldo Emerson

∾

It is in pardoning that we are pardoned.

~ Saint Francis of Assisi

∾

Whatever is begun in anger ends in shame.

~ Benjamin Franklin

∾

You give but little when you give of your possessions. It is when you give of yourself that you truly give.

~ Kahlil Gibran

∾

Never bend your head, always hold it high. Look the world straight in the eye.

~ Helen Keller

∾

Be happy for this moment. This moment is your life.

~ *Omar Khayyám*

Ɔ

The ability to be in the present moment is a major component
of mental wellness.

~ *Abraham Maslow*

Ɔ

Happy is the man who has broken the chains which hurt the
mind, and has given up worrying once and for all.

~ *Ovid*

Ɔ

Do not speak of your happiness to one less fortunate than yourself.

~ *Plutarch*

Ɔ

If there is harmony in the home, there will be order in the nation.
If there is order in the nation, there will be peace in the world.

~ *Chinese Proverb*

You may find the worst enemy or best friend within yourself.

~ *English Proverb*

A good cry lightens the heart.

~ *Yiddish Proverb*

Ɔ

Love consists in this, that two solitudes
protect and touch and greet each other.

~ *Rainer Maria Rilke*

∞

It isn't enough to talk about peace. One must believe in it. And
it isn't enough to believe in it. One must work at it.

~ *Eleanor Roosevelt*

∞

Happiness is not having what you want, but wanting what you
have.

~ *Hyman Judah Schachtel*

∞

O Lord, that lends me life,
Lend me a heart replete with thankfulness!

~ *William Shakespeare*

Neither a borrower, nor a lender be;
For loan oft loses both itself and friend,
And borrowing dulls the edge of husbandry.
This above all: to thine own self be true,
And it must follow, as the night the day,
Thou canst not then be false to any man.

~ *William Shakespeare*

∞

Nothing contributes so much to tranquilize the
mind as a steady purpose—a point on which the
soul may fix its intellectual eye.

~ Mary Shelley

☙

What can be added to the happiness of a man who is in health,
out of debt, and has a clear conscience?

~ Adam Smith

☙

Peace begins with a smile.

~ Mother Teresa

☙

You must live in the present, launch yourself on every wave,
find your eternity in each moment.

~ Henry David Thoreau

Our life is frittered away by detail...Simplify, simplify.

~ Henry David Thoreau

☙

When God shuts a door, He opens a window.

~ Author Unknown

When I am anxious it is because I am living in the future.
When I am depressed it is because I am living in the past.

~ Author Unknown

∽

We can only be said to be alive in those moments when our
hearts are conscious of our treasures.

~ Thornton Wilder

∽

Success is peace of mind which is a direct result of self-
satisfaction in knowing you did your best to become
the best you are capable of becoming.

~ John Wooden

Success

***

I count him braver who overcomes his desires than him who conquers his enemies; for the hardest victory is over self.

~ *Aristotle*

One important key to success is self-confidence. An important key to self-confidence is preparation.

~ *Arthur Ashe*

Don't be afraid to give your best to what seemingly are small jobs. Every time you conquer one it makes you that much stronger. If you do the little jobs well, the big ones will tend to take care of themselves.

~ *Dale Carnegie*

The price of greatness is responsibility.

~ *Winston Churchill*

One is not born a woman, one becomes one.

~ Simone de Beauvoir

∾

I dwell in Possibility—
A fairer House than Prose—
More numerous of Windows—
Superior—for Doors—

~ Emily Dickinson

∾

Genius is one percent inspiration and ninety-nine
percent perspiration.

~ Thomas Edison

The three great essentials to achieve anything worth while are,
first, hard work; second, stick-to-itiveness;
third, common sense.

~ Thomas Edison

∾

It's never too late to become what you might have been.

~ George Eliot

∾

What lies behind us and what lies before us are tiny matters
compared to what lies within us.

~ Ralph Waldo Emerson

Do not go where the path may lead, go instead where there is no path and leave a trail.

~ *Ralph Waldo Emerson*

To laugh often and much; to win the respect of intelligent people and the affection of children...to leave the world a bit better...to know even one life has breathed easier because you have lived. This is to have succeeded.

~ *Ralph Waldo Emerson*

∽

I want to go on living after my death! And that's why I'm so grateful to God for having given me this gift, which I can use to develop myself and to express all that's inside me!

~ *Anne Frank*

∽

How do you get to Carnegie Hall? Practice!

~ *Jascha Heifitz*

∽

Think twice before you speak, because your words and influence will plant the seed of either success or failure in the mind of another.

~ *Napoleon Hill*

∽

Life is either a daring adventure or nothing.

~ Helen Keller

When we do the best that we can, we never know what miracle
is wrought in our life, or in the life of another.

~ Helen Keller

∞

I will prepare and some day my chance will come.

~ Abraham Lincoln

∞

The price of success is hard work, dedication to the job at hand,
and the determination that whether we win or lose, we have
applied the best of ourselves to the task at hand.

~ Vince Lombardi

∞

Trust no Future, howe'er pleasant!
Let the dead Past bury its dead!
Act,–act in the living Present!
Heart within, and God o'erhead.

~ Henry Wadsworth Longfellow

Perseverance is a great element of success. If you only
knock long enough and loud enough at the gate, you
are sure to wake up somebody.

~ Henry Wadsworth Longfellow

∞

Where there's a will there's a way.

~ Proverb

∾

If you count all your assets, you always show a profit.

~ Robert Quillen

∾

You gain strength, courage, and confidence by every experience in which you really stop to look fear in the face...You must do the thing you think you cannot do."

~ Eleanor Roosevelt

∾

Far better is it to dare mighty things, to win glorious triumphs, even though checkered by failure... than to rank with those poor spirits who neither enjoy much nor suffer much, because they live in a gray twilight that knows not victory nor defeat.

~ Theodore Roosevelt

∾

Dance, when you're broken open. Dance, if you've torn the bandage off. Dance in the middle of the fighting. Dance in your blood. Dance when you're perfectly free.

~ Rumi

∾

Go confidently in the direction of your dreams. Live the life
you have imagined.

~ Henry David Thoreau

∾

To succeed in life, you need two things:
ignorance and confidence.

~ Mark Twain

My life has been filled with terrible misfortunes—most of
which never happened.

~ Mark Twain

∾

You have achieved success if you have lived well, laughed
often and loved much.

~ Author Unknown

Wisdom

ornament

Memory is the mother of all wisdom.

~ Aeschylus

A prudent question is one-half of wisdom.

~ Francis Bacon

Learning sleeps and snores in libraries, but
wisdom is everywhere, wide awake, on tiptoe.

~ Josh Billings

A man begins cutting his wisdom teeth the first
time he bites off more than he can chew.

~ Herb Caen

Common sense in an uncommon degree is what
the world calls wisdom.

~ *Samuel Taylor Coleridge*

∽

By three methods we may learn wisdom: First,
by reflection, which is noblest; Second, by imitation,
which is easiest; and Third by experience, which
is the bitterest.

~ *Confucius*

∽

Wise men are not wise at all hours.

~ *Ralph Waldo Emerson*

∽

He is a wise man who does not grieve for the things
which he has not, but rejoices for those which he has.

~ *Epictetus*

∽

Cleverness is not wisdom.

~ *Euripides*

∽

Wisdom consists not so much in knowing what to do in the ultimate as in knowing what to do next.

~ Herbert Hoover

∾

Every man is a damn fool for at least five minutes every day; wisdom consists in not exceeding the limit.

~ Elbert Hubbard

∾

He dares to be a fool, and that is the first step in the direction of wisdom.

~ James Huneker

∾

It is astonishing with how little wisdom mankind can be governed, when that little wisdom is its own.

~ William Ralph Inge

∾

Honesty is the first chapter in the book of wisdom.

~ Thomas Jefferson

He who knows most, knows best how little he knows.

~ Thomas Jefferson

∾

Never does nature say one thing and wisdom another.

~ Juvenal

∞

It requires wisdom to understand wisdom: the music is nothing
if the audience is deaf.

~ Walter Lippmann

∞

Does wisdom perhaps appear on the earth as a raven which is
inspired by the smell of carrion?

~ Friedrich Nietzsche

∞

We don't receive wisdom; we must discover it for ourselves after
a journey that no one can take for us or spare us.

~ Marcel Proust

∞

The only journey is the one within.

~ Rainer Maria Rilke

∞

No one can make you feel inferior without your consent.

~ Eleanor Roosevelt

∞

Nine-tenths of wisdom is being wise in time.

~ *Theodore Roosevelt*

∾

To conquer fear is the beginning of wisdom.

~ *Bertrand Russell*

∾

Men are wise in proportion, not to their experience, but to their capacity for experience.

~ *George Bernard Shaw*

∾

The only true wisdom is in knowing you know nothing.

~ *Socrates*

Wonder is the beginning of wisdom.

~ *Socrates*

∾

Knowledge comes, but wisdom lingers.

~ *Alfred Lord Tennyson*

∾

It is a characteristic of wisdom not to do desperate things.

~ *Henry David Thoreau*

All good things are wild and free.

~ Henry David Thoreau

All this worldly wisdom was once the unamiable heresy of some
wise man.

~ Henry David Thoreau

It is wisdom to know others;
It is enlightenment to know one's self.

~ Lao Tzu

Appendices

Appendix: Favorite Quotes

Quote:_____

_____

_____

Quote:_____

_____

_____

Quote:_____

_____

_____

Quote:_____

_____

_____

Quote:_____

_____

_____

Quote: _____

_____

_____

Appendix: Gratitude Checklist

Accomplishments
I am grateful for …

_____

_____

_____

_____

_____

_____

_____

_____

Blessings
I am grateful for …

_____

_____

_____

_____

_____

_____

_____

_____

Events
I am grateful for ...

_____
_____
_____
_____
_____
_____
_____
_____

Family
I am grateful for ...

_____
_____
_____
_____
_____
_____
_____
_____

Freedom
I am grateful for ...

_____
_____
_____
_____
_____
_____
_____
_____

Friendships
I am grateful for …

_____

_____

_____

_____

_____

_____

_____

Gifts
I am grateful for …

_____

_____

_____

_____

_____

_____

_____

Little Things
I am grateful for …

_____

_____

_____

_____

_____

_____

_____

Significant Moments
I am grateful for ...

_____

_____

_____

_____

_____

_____

_____

_____

Success
I am grateful for ...

_____

_____

_____

_____

_____

_____

_____

_____

Things I Never Expected
I am grateful for ...

_____

_____

_____

_____

_____

_____

_____

_____

Other
I am grateful for …

_____

_____

_____

_____

_____

_____

_____

_____

_____

_____

_____

_____

_____

_____

_____

_____

_____

_____

_____

_____

_____

_____

_____

_____

Appendix: Gratitude Journal

January: _____

_____

_____

_____

_____

_____

_____

_____

_____

_____

February: _____

_____

_____

_____

_____

_____

_____

_____

_____

_____

March: _____

_____

_____

_____

_____

_____

_____

_____

_____

_____

April: _____

_____

_____

_____

_____

_____

_____

_____

_____

May: _____

_____

_____

_____

_____

_____

_____

_____

_____

June: _____

_____

_____

_____

_____

_____

_____

_____

_____

_____

July: _____

_____

_____

_____

_____

_____

_____

_____

_____

August: _____

_____

_____

_____

_____

_____

_____

_____

_____

September: _____

_____

_____

_____

_____

_____

_____

_____

_____

_____

October: _____

_____

_____

_____

_____

_____

_____

_____

_____

November: _____

_____

_____

_____

_____

_____

_____

_____

_____

December: _____

_____

_____

_____

_____

_____

_____

_____

_____

_____

Biographical Index

Aeschylus: 525-456 BC, Greek playwright
Alcott, Louisa May: 1832-1888, American novelist
Aristotle: 384-322 BC, Greek philosopher
Ashe, Arthur: 1943-1993, American professional tennis player
Aurelius, Marcus: 121-180, Roman Emperor

Bacon, Francis: 1561-1626, English philosopher
Beecher, Henry Ward: 1813-1887, American clergyman
Bell, Alexander Graham: 1847-1922, American inventor
Bibesco, Elizabeth: 1897-1945, English writer
Billings, Josh: 1818-1885, American writer
Blake, William: 1757-1827, English poet
Blyth, Reginald Horace: 1898-1964, English author
Brecht, Bertolt: 1898-1956, German poet and playwright
Brontë, Charlotte: 1816-1855, English novelist and poet
Browning, Elizabeth Barrett: 1806-1861, English poet
Browning, Robert: 1812-1889, English poet
Buck, Pearl S. (Sydenstricker): 1892-1973, American writer
Buddha: 563-483 BC, Spiritual teacher
Burns, Robert: 1759-1796, Scottish poet
Buscaglia, Felice Leonardo "Leo": 1924-1998: American author and lecturer

Caen, Herb: 1916-1997: American newspaper columnist
Canning, George: 1770-1827, British politician
Carnegie, Dale: 1888-1955, American writer and lecturer
Chapin, Edwin Hubbell: 1814-1880, American preacher
Chesterton, G.K. (Gilbert Keith): 1874-1936, English author
Churchill, Winston: 1874-1965, British politician
Cicero: 106-43 BC, Roman philosopher
Clay, Henry: 1777-1852, American statesman
Coleridge, Samuel Taylor: 1772-1834, English poet
Colman, George: 1762-1836, English writer
Confucius: 551-479 BC, Chinese philosopher
Cousins, Margaret: 1905-1996, American writer

de Beauvoir, Simone: 1908-1986, French writer
de Benneville, George: 1703-1793, French physician
Dickens, Charles: 1812-1870, English novelist
Dickinson, Emily: 1830-1886, American poet
Disraeli, Benjamin: 1804-1881, British Prime Minister
Doyle, Sir Arthur Conan: 1859-1930, Scottish physician and writer
Drucker, Peter: 1909-2005, American writer and management consultant
Dryden, John: 1631-1700, English poet

Eckhart, Meister: 1260-1327, German philosopher
Edison, Thomas: 1847-1931, American inventor
Einstein, Albert: 1879-1955, German-Swiss scientist
Eliot, George (Mary Ann Evans): 1819-1880, English novelist
Eliot, T.S. (Thomas Stearns): 1888-1965, American poet
Emerson, Ralph Waldo: 1803-1882, American writer and poet
Epictetus: 55-135, Greek philosopher
Euripedes: 480-406 BC, Greek playwright

Francis of Assisi, Saint: 1181-1226, Italian preacher
Faulkner, William, 1897-1962, American writer

Frank, Anne: 1929-1945, German writer
Franklin, Benjamin: 1706-1790, American author and statesman
Frost, Robert: 1874-1963, American poet
Fromm, Erich: 1900-1980, German writer and social psychologist

Gandhi, Mahatma: 1869-1948, Indian political leader
Gibran, Kahlil: 1883-1931, Lebanese American writer and poet
Goethe, Johann Wolfgang von: 1749-1832, German writer

Haley, Alex: 1921-1992, African-American writer
Hawthorne, Nathaniel: 1804-1864, American writer
Heifitz, Jascha: 1901-1987, Russian violinist
Henley, William Ernest: 1849-1903, English poet
Hepburn, Katherine: 1907-2003, American actress
Herbert, George: 1593-1633, Welsh poet
Hill, Napoleon: 1883-1970, American writer
Hoffer, Eric: 1902-1983, American writer and philosopher
Hoover, Herbert: 1874-1964, American President of the United States
Horace: 65-8 BC, Roman philosopher
Hubbard, Elbert: 1856-1915, American writer
Huneker, James: 1860-1921, American music writer and critic
Huxley, Aldous: 1864-1963, English writer

Inge, William Ralph: 1860-1954, English author

Jefferson, Thomas: 1743-1826, American President of the United States
Jung, Karl: 1875-1961, Swiss psychiatrist
Juvenal: 55-138, Roman poet

Keats, John: 1795-1821, English poet
Keller, Helen: 1880-1968, American writer
Kennedy, John Fitzgerald: 1917-1963, American President of the United States

Khayyám, Omar: 1048-1131, Persian poet
King, Basil: 1859-1928, Canadian writer
King, Jr., Martin Luther: 1929-1968, American clergyman
Kipling, Rudyard: 1865-1936, English writer
Krisnamurti, Jiddu: 1895-1986, Indian writer

la Rouchefoucauld, François, Duc de: 1613-1680, French writer
Lazarus, Emma: 1849-1887, American poet
Lincoln, Abraham: 1809-1865, American President of the United States
Lombardi, Vince: 1913-1970, Italian-American football coach
Lippmann, Walter: 1889-1974, American writer
Longfellow, Henry Wadsworth: 1807-1882, American poet

Maslow, Abraham: 1908-1970, American professor of psychology
Miller, Henry: 1891-1980, American writer and painter
Moore, Marianne: 1887-1972, American poet

Newton, John: 1725-1807, English clergyman
Niebuhr, Reinhold: 1892-1971, American theologian
Nietzsche, Friedrich: 1844-1900, German philosopher

O'Keefe, Georgia: 1887-1986, American artist
Olatunji, Babatunde: 1927-2003, Nigerian drummer
Ovid: 43 BC-17 AD, Roman poet

Plato: 428-348 BC, Greek philosopher
Plutarch: 46-120, Greek historian
Pope, Alexander: 1688-1744, English poet
Porter, Katherine Anne: 1890-1980, American writer
Proust, Marcel: 1871-1922, French novelist
Purkiser, W.T.: 1910-1992, American writer

Quillen, Robert: 1887-1948, American writer

Rilke, Rainer Maria: 1875-1926, Austrian poet
Robinson, Edwin Arlington: 1869-1935, American poet
Rossetti, Christina: 1830-1894, English poet
Roosevelt, Eleanor: 1884-1962, American writer and First Lady of the United States
Roosevelt, Theodore: 1858-1919, American President of the United States
Rumi: 1207-1273, Persian poet
Russell, Bertrand: 1872-1970, British philosopher

Schachtel, Hyman Judah: 1907-1990, American Rabbi
Schweitzer, Albert: 1875-1965, Franco-German theologian
Dr. Seuss (Theodor Seuss Giesel): 1904-1991, American writer
Shakespeare, William: 1564-1616, English poet and playwright
Shaw, George Bernard: 1856-1950, Irish playwright
Shelley, Mary (Mary Wollstonecraft Godwin): 1797-1851, English writer
Smith, Adam: 1723-1790, Scottish philosopher
Socrates: 469-399 BC, Greek philosopher
South, Robert: 1634-1716, English speaker and writer
Stern, G.B. (Gladys Bronwyn): 1890-1973, English writer
Stevenson, Robert Louis: 1850-1894, Scottish novelist and poet

Tagore, Rabindranath: 1861-1941, Bengali poet
Tennyson, Alfred Lord: 1809-1892, English poet and writer
Teresa, Mother: 1910-1997, Albanian nun
Thoreau, Henry David: 1817-1862, American writer and poet
Tolstoy, Leo: 1828-1910, Russian writer
Twain, Mark (Samuel Langhorne Clemens): 1835-1910, American writer
Tzu, Lao: 570-490 BC, Chinese philosopher

Virgil: 70-19 BC, Roman poet
Voltaire: 1694-1778, French writer

Ward, William Arthur: 1921-1994, American writer
Wattles, Wallace: 1860-1911, American writer
Whitman, Walt: 1819-1892, American poet
Wilcox, Ella Wheeler: 1850-1919, American writer and poet
Wilde, Oscar: 1854-1900, Irish writer
Wilder, Thornton: 1897-1975, American playwright
Wooden, John: 1910-2010, American basketball coach
Wordsworth, William: 1770-1850, English poet

Yeats, William Butler: 1865-1939, Irish poet

Biographical Index

Kathleen Welton has developed award-winning books, series, and Websites while working with the American Bar Association, Dearborn Trade, IDG Books, and Rowman & Littlefield. *100 Essential Modern Poems by Women*, co-edited with Joseph Parisi, was selected as a Benjamin Franklin Award Finalist in 2009 and *Poetry for Beginners*, co-authored with Margaret Chapman, was published in 2010. She studied English and Italian literature at Stanford University before becoming an editor and publishing professional.

CPSIA information can be obtained at www.ICGtesting.com
Printed in the USA
LVOW081527131112

307156LV00012B/82/P

9 780578 065861